The Garden of My Verses

Mon Maya Mongar

 pencil

ISBN 978-93-5610-677-2
© Mon Maya Mongar 2022
Published in India 2022 by Pencil

Contributors:
Editor: Ignatius Maximus John

A brand of
One Point Six Technologies Pvt. Ltd.
123, Building J2, Shram Seva Premises,
Wadala Truck Terminal, Wadala (E)
Mumbai 400037, Maharashtra, INDIA
E connect@thepencilapp.com
W www.thepencilapp.com

Author biography

Mon Maya Mongar is a righteous and reasonable young poetess from Bhutan. She was born on 2nd March 1999 and grew up at the wonderful place known as Nimtola, Dagana. Her parents are both reputable farmers who supported her education adequately. She completed her primary education from Nimtola Primary School and Secondary education from Gesarling Central School. She graduated her higher studies from Daga Central School in the year 2019 and currently pursuing B.A in Bhutanese and Himalayan Studies at the College of Language and Culture Studies.

She is also a passionate writer since her school-going days. Writing and expressing through poetry gave her eternal satisfaction and her undying love for poetry bestowed her knowledge beyond bound. Moreover, her immortal devotion to poetry and literature has blessed her with considerable certificates, recognition, and appreciation from various international poetry platforms.

Nevertheless, her poems have been published in numerous international anthologies and magazines such as The Continental Anthology of Contemporary African Poetry,

Motivational Strips, Poetry Planet International Magazine (January 2022, edition), and Poetry Planet International Magazine (February 2022 edition).

CONTENTS

Epigraph

Garden of feelings

That someone can sing

Sometimes sorrow it can bring

Otherwise, can heal the internal suffering.

Garden of beauty

Impressions of honesty

The joy of an acceptability

With immortal bless of almighty.

Preface

My fondness for writing thrived after every second and as a young writer, I always dreamt about earning a published author's badge. I jot down anything that my mind interrogated, views that my eyes witnessed, sound that my ears collected, and insight that my heart and brain reflected. I kept on scribbling without a rigid theme. Therefore, this poetry book is named " The Garden Of My Verses". It doesn't maintain any hidden meaning but the poetry garden acts as my verse's frame.

Just like hundreds of flowers can bloom in a garden, I consider this book as a glorious garden that comprises diverse poetry verses including romance, philosophy, spirituality, humanity, nature, culture, and tradition.

"Ohh, garden
Please don't get burdened
For I am planting my verses
Not the flowers of dears".

Mon Maya Mongar
Dagana, Bhutan
20th March 2022

Dedication

This book is dedicated to my parents and my only brother

Aroma of Love

When your tipsy sight

Lingers around me,

My ordinary nerves earn to tickle,

I could sense but can't see,

A slight glimpse of that

Beautifies my sickening mood,

Which generates me to crave for

Heart's aromatic duet.

Infinite contentment activates

Crawls into my love vision,

Just with a glance,

The fragrance of affection commences

Flowing in my imagination,

Your considerable smile

Took away my breathe,

Even though I was unaware,

Everything between us continued to be great.

I want to sow the seed

Of affection in your heart,

With which we can tie our bond

And shall never depart,

Let the birds appreciate our togetherness and sing,

And be our witness that sky brings.

You are the most treasured artifact in my hearts museum,

Which I only enroll my heart for fusion,

Devoid of your presence,

My heart knows no melody,

Let this cosmic devotion dance

With our love symphony.

Street Dweller

Ohh, God!

Is this his only destiny?

Happiness? Not even once,

He hasn't celebrated its ceremony,

Around, he beholds the world of the symphony,

But it's altered,

His fate has been elaborated with agony.

Until the dawn gets to rise,

Street light assisted to become

His neighbor's prize,

His arms tried hard

To protect his head from mud,

Laying his body on the scraps

Under the tree, he could discern birds on the tree buds.

Street children became his family,

Couldn't help each other

But had to strive for self breathlessly,

A sip of water would mean a lot,

But even the sky betrayed him,

Rain without a drop.

The scorching rays burned his skin,

His dream to get the shadow

Under the umbrella has just been,

The fallen leaves fell as his blanket,

But the shade of a tree just left when the autumn fetched.

All that abides around him was a stranger,

Even the existing earth,

When people passed by he craved,

But a maximum of them forgot to recognize him, beneath,

People who did gave him once or twice

But never thrice,

Squeezing his stomach, begging, and digging the bins

Has cut his existence into slices.

Many years passed by and still,

He couldn't move,

It means like,

He became a street dweller to prove,

Not for the fate for fortunate doom,

But for unpredictable gloom.

Sorrowful Soul

The day you veered
Your affection forever
I found I was just breathing
In your possibility,
That potential of waiting
Went on and on,
Like history,
Just remained with mystery.

Yet, I still don't know
Why I was abandoned,
But the creations of scars
You painted haunted me every second,
Those glamorous memories
Whirled into grievous stories,
Sometimes wakes me up with
Dreadful agonies.

Multiple sleepless nights
Were gone,
And I am still with the pretender smile
With the world,
My feeling commenced becoming
A hollow,
That I am thought alive but
Extinct inside.

Desolate emotion hauled me
Continuously,
Over time,
I lost my contentment completely,
I became like a wood, that prevails,
With the beauty of nature
But it's already dead.

I subsisted with swoon,
More with confusion,
Ultimately,
I yearned to be alone,
Every night with the solitary feeling,
The glittering moon encouraged me
To spend my solitude.

Gifted Gift

Would not have been this earth,
I would have fallen beneath,
When I just stepped down,
From mother's womb to this massive ground.

Would not have been the sun,
Blindness would have assisted me to go insane,
Still with open eyes,
But holding vague belief where the sky lies.

Would not have been the gentle winds,
Its generous ebb would not have pampered my thick mind,
High in the sky, fly kites
I would not have known, plays by the kids.

Would not have been the flower blooms
Its blossoms would yet have remained in the gloom,
The land of extreme,
The planet would ultimately become.

Would not have been the tree,

The direct rays would have radiated me,

Intensely without its existence of cool shadow,

Even while walking in a vast meadow.

Woman Beside The Road

The sun was already overhead,

I was walking to cross the road,

There, my eyes caught a woman,

She seemed lost with hallucination.

She was broken and shattered,

All her dreams are dead and scattered,

She was waiting desperately,

In both thunder and storm lowly.

"Please God answer her", I thought to myself,

Everyone has obstacles to overcome themselves,

I say," God is unfair",

She is in despair.

A big truck with a load appeared,

As I watch them, my heart got sophisticated,

The driver in the truck was busy talking,

Towards him, I saw woman suddenly running.

Without atrophying, I ran,
I pulled her beside me as much as I can,
She fell in my arm,
It was more like a dream.

The neighbor came instantly,
I was relieved to see her safe, gladly,
The neighbor told, "She lost her child here",
I realized she was living her life in a nightmare.

You Are My Inspiration

In times of sorrow,

In doubt about where the future would take me,

Someone heard me right,

With the sunrise,

He grabbed my hand,

Pointing faraway moving clouds under the cool blue sky,

He marked the trail,

I wondered who would that be?

A guardian sent from heaven?

When I stepped down the treat,

The scene blends bliss and traffic,

All in tears of dilemma,

I broke down to the bottom,

I lost every hope a person owns.

It was hot midday, I met with an unknown,

He chose to be my shadow,

I again wondered, who would that be?

A missioned angel?

Bringing in every step and faded dream,

In those journeys of the dead,

I was lost with all my energy,

Someone encountered my way.

When the cold evening arrived, he came along.

I again wondered, who would that be?

Was he my friend?

Ever since I encountered the guardian sent from heaven,

Ever since I encountered the missioned angel,

Ever since I encountered an unknown friend,

My determination grew like morning sunshine.

The brighter it grew, the more purity it showed.

He who held my hand,

The right destination, he showed.

He who became my shadow,

He gave me safety.

He who became my friend,

When all abandoned me, he remained.

Those lighters are my teachers.

Thank you all the geniuses,

For letting me be real,

For leading me to be where I belong,

And still leading to the wonderful land of aspiration.

Like the leaves subsides because the fall arrives,

I may break down time and again.

But I'm strong,

Because you are my real inspiration.

When I fall,

I fear reaching the bare ground.

But your words I have,

I can pull up my nerves.

Like togetherness,

I admired your attitude,

I admired your values,

I admired your education,

And still, I admire your inspiration.

Within this deep ocean heart,

I wish every sunrise and sunset

Brings birth to a teacher.

A teacher who brings surprises,

A teacher who implants wisdom,

A teacher who sows the seed of curiosity and motivation,

Someday, I hope to be a teacher.

A teacher who would imprint the greatness in one's life,

Just like what you left in my heart.

Accept Life As It Is

Life is an unreachable journey,
Everyone should walk,
Nothing can be considered permanent,
One day I should die, you should die.

Life is indescribable,
Sometimes unstoppable laugh appears,
Wide opened mouth, a fragile smile
Sometimes a piece of misery breaks out,
Which destroys the way to our destination.

A sack full of happiness, a pocketful of peace,
And handful smiles.
Even a tiny joy becomes just a memory,
Feels as if it can appear again,
An unexpected incident happens,
For it let us accept and deny it.

The way towards a never-ending journey,

With a sorrowful soul,
And joyful happiness attached,
Take it easy, life is crazy.

Silence

When the sun drives

Behind the mountain,

The crescent moon crawls up,

Little bright stars glitter,

while the sea stays so calm.

When I have tones to say

But can't,

My heart aches and

Wants to whimper,

when everyone turns their back to me,

I miss the silence.

The crescent moon glances at me,

As I watch up the shiny sky,

The wind gently

And softly touches my cheek,

Asking me how do I feel.

The boat near the sea dwells in static,

I climb on it and

Feel the flow,

The night stays so cool,

I get lost and feel like a fool.

Lockdown

COVID -19 is the reason for lockdown,

It has been quite a period and it already makes me frown,

The longer it chooses to be with us,

Emptiness will replenish our glamorous campus.

It's fetching hard to boost a smile,

But I believe, it's just for a while,

The leaders are striving for their best,

And we should exist as the strongest.

Never we should reckon,

Lockdown is like a prison,

It's the best weapon to combat,

It's already on our door, so do not react.

Of course, we lost everything,

Jobs and money we could still be earning,

But why won't we realize?

If we are safe today, tomorrow will finalize.

Family is what we should clench in our heart,

At this crucial point of life, we should never be apart,

Let's hold our close ones by our side,

And let them know the consequences with our adequate
guide.

Let's stay home with our family and pray,

Pinpoint safety first and do not forget to wear a mask
every day,

Together we wish, to let this curse vanish,

And let peace and prosperity accomplish.

Poetic Sight

My only mind, my only heart,

From poetry, it cannot be apart,

The view which I gradually spot at,

My heart and mind adore it when I wear the poetry hat.

That clean lying dewdrops,

Tickles my inner nerve to drop,

The ink on tremendous verses,

That's when my fantasy crosses.

The rising dawn, I glimpse,

My lyric says it's a natural glamorous

That would never collapse,

Warm golden rays,

Through the fleshes and bones it penetrates.

As I walk along the path,

I discern I am taking a poetry bath,

I never stop wishing the joy,

That even without wings, I am jogging in the sky.

When the thunder growls and hailstone falls,

I don't know what others does, but my hand with the pen crawls,

It must be horrible the situation is,

But my brain never enters to freeze.

Illusion and delusion, I wear poetic spectacle,

The poetic option, I behold from every angle,

The misery and paradise I can indeed foresee,

I am even powered to bring back that gone glee.

Little Lucky Charm

Oh, little prince,

You stepped into this nation's mud

With massive grace,

Most awaited by creatures

And peoples' fate,

It was never too late and

You unlocked the door of security

And fortune-owning gate.

Oh, little prince,

Your presence completed my heart's space,

Born with eternal compassion and elegance,

Tickled every nature aspect

To bring glorious fragrance.

Oh, little prince,

Your magnificent face,

Like the charitable mother moon,

Even in the darkness,

Your appearance provokes every aspect to bloom.

Oh, little prince,

On this joyous edge,

I wish you extended life and a healthy badge.

Solitary Gaze

The midnight has completely gained,
Every creature was asleep
But I was awake, frightened!
The stillness prevailed,
Pin-drop silence,
Holding shaken, shattered, and betrayed heart
I glimpsed up to the moon
And suddenly caught a glance.

Still with a sorrowful soul,
Existing with a deserted sensation,
I lifted my head with realization,
Entire relaxation that I stood with the moon,
I believed the moon was lonely
Yet like her, I am going to serve soon.

Under the vastness of the sky,
I asked myself not to cry,
Because the motherly moon

Gazed at me with her compassionate eye,
And it was true, never a lie.

The sun evacuated the light
When dusk arrived,
Hiding all my despair with the daylight,
I passionately waited
For the dawn to derive,
The emerging moon gave me a
Great delight,
I felt fortunate that even in the darkness,
I was under the moonlight.

The moonlight took away
The misery and agony I hold,
I got to breathe the air of relief
Relying on the motherly moon to behold,
Thereon solitary left me
Unknowingly,
Without recognition,
I was able to smile gracefully.

Undying Love

I watched the sky above

And thanked the heaven

For we are still together

By her grace and blessing.

Never I dreamt

That we would be,

Never I imagined

Your devotion will melt me.

Never I thought

I would get lost,

Nowhere, but just in your

Glossy smile,

I feel fortunate,

Of all women

That I am the crowned queen

Not others, but yours

Never you were harsh

But ever, flowed with the flow.

Ohh, God, I shall never beg

Any more than this

That I could swim

Only in his ocean lust.

Hey, love,

Those twinkling stars,

We counted together

Glory motherly moon,

We felt together,

High, higher the sky

We flew

And viewed those glamorous beauties.

You were the might

You were the light

And you brought abundance dance of delight

The Cruel War

Why should I jot down

When the mentality of

People are still

Connected with insanity.

They never realized

To boost their only affection,

Circulate their generosity

But regardless, focused on cruelty.

Yesterday, everything was regular

But today, found nonexistent

Someone close to the heart,

Their loved ones are found breathless,

Their houses are burned down,

Everything was left behind

With complete misery and agony.

No one would have even dreamt

The cruelty they had to face

Just after they unlock their eyes.

This terrific earth became

The ego land for leaders
They enjoyed wearing away innocent ones.
The destination they targeted,
Dreams they fixed,
And jobs they secured,
All these vanished with the smoky air,
With the sound of guns,
With their sorrowful tears.
Nowhere, the fresh air is
Nowhere, did the birds singing
Nowhere, the water is clean
Nowhere, the wind is gentle
Nowhere, the love and smile
But all replenished with unbearable grief.

Happy Birthday

O, heaven, bless him

Today is the day he became

O, fairy fulfill his wishes

He is a man of wisdom

Never he was harsh,

But always filled with friendliness

He is a man of literature

Who he keeps on roaring ahead

Coz he only believes to change

Both his view

And the world of distraction.

O, golden rays,

Let him shine with you

Never let him follow

the darkness

Coz that doesn't suit him

He wears the coat of light

Which eventually twinkles brightly

His eyes are filled with charity

Which holds the

best viewpoint.

O, gentle wind,

Give him the pampering flow

Let his heart enrich with

Striking love.

Let its flow let him

Forget all his gained sorrow.

O, God

I assure you

You won't regret

For his existence

For he is worth existing.

Birthday Wish

On this day

you were found and stood

on this blessed ground,

You fulfilled those years

with reasonable amusement

but had to even bear with certain disappointment,

You encountered unlimited

life's disasters,

And declared you are

your own master,

Anyhow, another year of exhilaration,

With your enthusiastic motion,

You shall fruitfully spend it,

You shall not waste it.

Wish Her

Dear men, draw your pen to cheer up your women,
Not the swords and cruelty to bruise her emotion,

She never gets tired of stretching a bridge
Can't you just spend a second to message?

She must be dying to hear your wishes,
As she reckons, she has a man to miss.

With the opening of dawn, call your mom,
Being pleased for becoming such a heavenly bloom.

Open your message box and text your sister,
For always occurring as a great supporter.

Write a letter to your daughter,
For invariably evolving as an independent fighter.

Women's Day

If I don't hold a pen today,

My heart and soul will surely cry,

Crunch me within and lets me burn up,

Until the next women's day turns up.

Feel my verses, dear women

Realize and comprehend, dear gentlemen,

I guarantee, a man who cares will flip around,

But those who have hidden horns and claws will just fall
on the bound.

I say with pride, women are not just them,

They are existing profound gems,

Dear men, you have a genuine jewel,

Instead of measuring them, why do you always forward
them to fuel?

Women are the divine warrior,

Her strength is beyond yours,

She makes sure she attends everywhere,

But you open your mouth with zero care.

Why should women bear the societal threat?

It's obviously because men take women just as a piece of
bread,

When you maintain the vicious intention,

You are out of the honorable mention.

Women are the source of politeness,

If you try to drag her down, she purely focuses to bring
massive bitterness.

She subsists with the sword of heroism,

Always try to understand her mechanism.

Those who oversee will appreciate here,

Even if you blame me, I don't care,

Because these are the truth,

And I don't believe in that superstitious myth.

Twisted Love

Unknowingly it emerged as a love triangle,

Because our affectionate heart was so fragile,

The heavenly set we became,

We blindly fell upon it, but I assure you it's not a game.

Our past didn't exist,

And I even don't care about the philosophy of Marxists,

Just the reality of you at present shines,

I feel our love was designed as divine.

I maybe the bird of prey,

But let me watch you until you turn grey,

My wings desire to fly higher,

Which my eyes at you, a real fixer.

Love can be as sharp as a thin blade,

But love me the way I was initially made.

My Poetic Sister

We are still strangers but known from heart,

It's worth mentioning, that we shall never depart,

The mysterious poetry united us,

And with the affection of togetherness, the world greeted
us.

Dear sister, you are miles away,

But you reside in my heart, anyway,

When the soothing wind blows,

I imagine, your heartful message to me pleasantly flows.

Your smile defines you are highly generous,

I would say, you are a woman of fluke with no rigorous,

That friendship propels me to feel great,

It commonly inspires me to get away with any threat.

Your heart filled with affection,

With no differentiation, but to everyone with enthusiasm,

I could see encouragement and positivity in your eyes,

Though you hold sadness within, your determination lies
above the sky.

Dear heavenly god,

I feel grateful, that you sent her here to celebrate her
angelhood,

Worth existing, the earth is blessed,

Not only me, I see everyone is interested

Two-Faced Love

Love is a ray of light

If you handle it,

It will shine luminously,

Mysterious sight it will furnish,

Those eyes keeps on crawling.

The specialty of affection

Turns into golden wings,

Which will eventually energies you to fly high

Above the sky,

Even the raindrops bestows

You the calmness,

Everything you see around

Feels like a blessing.

You can't quit smiling,

The mind can't stop wavering,

Limbs keep on wanting to dance,

With your humming romantic songs,

Your imagination of pleasure and desire

Continues to flow like a river,

You make sure with yourself,

You can abstain

From everything you have,

The trust and utmost devotion

Shall be pinned,

If not love can ruin your goal,

You will surely get stuck,

Let's you lose everything

With a deserted feeling,

And the abandoned sense

Enjoys crunching your hearts and emotions,

It will shut down the rays

The hope and determination.

Those gone memories will haunt,

While nightmare walks after you,

Your realm co-exists with the gloom.

Seriously Blank

Why my mind reflects me blankly,

I don't remember, did I drink madly?

Nah, I didn't go to the shop since dawning,

And a week ago, my mom stopped alcohol fermenting.

Am I dreaming? Nah, I am just thinking,

Ohh no, I am not sure, or am I merely guessing?

I knew I was lost,

But where? Dust?

My belly is tight,

Did I push too much rice?

Did I insert from the right direction,

Ohh, sorry nose if I have done unfair action.

Have I gone insane? Feeling completely dizzy,

Everything seems up and down transmitting crazy,

What has gotten into me?

Insanity is hanging me near to the sky, but I don't feel free.

Ohh my God! I must be in illusion,

Creating foolish imagination,

Wanting to imagine more,

Sometimes, It's making my brain wildly sore.

Attitude

Attitude is when you have
A positive emotions and beliefs.
A manner your behavior shows,
And the tendency and orientation
You have towards something.

Everyone is endorsed with an attitude,
An attitude matters in everyone's life.
Attitude applies to every sphere of life,
both personal and professional.

Recognition is an attitude,
Accepting the fault is attitude.
Realizing your mistake,
And preferring the right opportunity is attitude.

Our attitude defines our lives,
A positive attitude holder
Gas a positive drive,

In all the thick and thin in his life,
All he can have is, win in thrive.

A negative one always gets resented,
The more he works,
The purposeless life he foresee,
An unpleasant environment is formed,
Indirectly it creates unnecessary stress.

To a person with a negative mind,
Life gives him obstacles.
The more he gets skeptical,
bitterness surrounds him.

We are comfortable with what we had,
But why change?
Gaining a positive one
Pays you complete success,
your pleasing personality
Fosters your surroundings.
Opportunity is never restricted,
So step into positivity and success.

Mighty Ink

You are rich because you ink,

No credit to pay, once more think,

Contribute through the pen,

Disseminate wisdom and awareness claiming attentive
gain,

The entire relaxation it provides being,

That your pen brushes away the feeling of agony and
eventually subsides,

No doubt, you will cheer up,

Holding vivid smiles, you will brighten up.

Plentiful you will serve,

Just sitting with a pen you will revolve,

Glimpsing the earthly nature,

Assuming the worldly future.

The vibrant perspective it shows,

From the instant, your pen begins to glow,

Your ink introduces you,

Everywhere, anytime to every individual delivering its soothing flow.

The Way We Were

Existing together on this detached earth,

We never got to know each other with its mysterious art,

Presence of those hilly areas, weird cliffs, and smooth
mountains,

Acted as a barrier for our foundations.

Yet, we were anonymous to each other.

I sighted the eastern sun before you,

And wished the moon good night, earlier the dark it grew,

But we greeted the same dawn rise,

And watched that brilliant moon with elegant eyes,

Unknowingly, you breathed near me.

Somehow, we got connected online,

Our initial greeting was extremely fine,

It prevailed with your pen of love rhyme,

While It extensively caught my heart which was never a
crime,

There, I was cheerfully drowned in your ink.

Your mighty ink brought us even nigher,

While I used to read late-night serving full attention payer,

I felt every word you penned was certainly for me,

And overjoyed your lines with abundant glee.

Then, you subsisted solely in my sanity.

Once, we were strangers but not now,

That magical pen united us somehow,

The existence of nature's terrific art didn't matter,

Thereon, we had purely attached,

Seriously, the distance didn't question me.

Saviour

He is a man of bravery,
Who wants what he desires which is extraordinary,
A heart filled with boldness and strength,
He doesn't know what he will do to breathe,
But one thing he wants is to be great.

He owns a delighted family,
A generous friend to spend time gracefully,
Creating memories with them was his fulfillment,
But when the World enters into discouragement,
He wants to be the world's protection.

He decides to join soldiers,
A protection shield to the country and,
become people's frontier,
He grows with an audacious heart,
To serve the country fight,
And one day prove his outstanding might.

The angel he meets,

Their love begins with a nice set,

Exchanging nimble smiles with the midnight moon,

Holding hands and hands to reach heavenly bloom,

They suit the incredible bride and groom.

He leaves his friends and family behind,

Letting near ones with waiting hopes in the homeland.

In his heart filled with sadness,

When she dwells with swollen eyes with his unforgotten
memories,

Their world of love gets to part beyond boundaries.

He fights the enemy courageously,

Hoping to bring everyone safe, prosperously,

He climbs the hilly mountain to reach the top,

Gun in his hand with lion eyes up,

Just to restore his country's bliss up.

He fights to the death,

At the very end, he arrives in a coffin box through a
footpath.

Family and dear ones are left in sorrow,

Bringing the country's luminous future tomorrow,

Finally, his recollection photo hangs on the walls in a row.

Rain Soothes My Pain

Yet winter is here, but I notice summer is dashing,
The winter dirt, stirring
Down the drain, formulating so refreshing
Everywhere is green and vitalizing.

The falling rain rises me believe, it's summer,
it's still here, the chilly cold winter,
When fiercely flowing winds gives a slight blow,
The cloudy mist reaps to lend a foggy glow.

While the hedges settle to receive the blessing drain,
I appreciate the mighty falling rain,
I could comprehend their relaxation,
After an extended cold dry winter creation.

A determined drop of rain falls from the high sky,
Eventually equips the bird to rejoice their fly,
And compels me to go foretold,
With falling droplets and the birds vocalizing, the best set.

Fated

More fortunate I feel our fate conspired

And our relationship is heavenly occupied,

Let's fly over to our destined destination

With enormous excitement and passionate affection,

Regardless of the rain which even brings hail,

But eventually gets to face the rainbow without fail,

To glance at you, my heart aches,

But when I can't uncover you, unknown depression it creates,

Let's create great memories,

Which is full of cheerful glories.

A Cup of Coffee

Every sip of coffee in the evening,
Makes me believe, that all my tiring feeling is leaving,
The dark color and slightly acidic it can be,
But ultimately brings a stimulating
effect in me.

As I hold a cup of coffee,
I am inclined to forget all the frustration and agony, free!
Consciously my nose catches its aroma faster than the air,
Which eventually makes me realize everything is now fair.

Automatically my eyes can't stop closing
When I take a sip, generates my heart so loose,
The flavor in my mouth remains unwiped,
Yet, provokes my lips with a prevailing interest.

With relaxation, I realize
Looking at dark coffee with a thorough gaze

"I drink dark but feels satisfactory,
Every dark do not release dark story".

Come On

Yes, dear, we are far

Not from heaven but I am from earth

Your smile is my satisfaction

Your sunshine is my sunshine

And that gives us a reason

To wake up every morning

Your affection fills me within

Even when nothing is well

I love you until the sky falls over

And even after the mud gets apart.

I Was Young

I was young but my mom never kept me inexperienced,

Before the sunrise I had to raise my head, determined,

To start the house chores with

And after dinner ends it with a tidy sweeping.

Holding new age, I was trained to be careful,

Sometimes messed up with scolding but taught to be
mindful,

That exclaiming wisdom was a lesson,

Now I realize, which a mother can authorize to her
daughter with eternal passion.

My childhood days were exclusively replenished,

With awesome vision and insight, completed,

That a girl shall proceed in her life throughout,

Which my mother was always uptight about.

Those remembrances still flicker vividly,

That I had to cook and feed my siblings awesomely,

But forgot to cook curry when mom is gone,

And unfortunately had to feed them the rice soup with
sane.

Those days seem to be depressing and awful,

Yet I still believe, my mom gave me her best, the choice of
beautiful,

I yearned to reap like other kids,

But I got it forthwith I had wisdom the entire childhood.

Ill-Fated Love

Those mists attracted my sight,
But got to hide beside the hills,
I trusted those snows on the peaks,
Still it melt with the sun.

A fortune designed to depart,
Was never made to succeed,
Though felt by the heart,
But contradicted by its destiny.

In my garden of the feeling,
You bloomed as a lotus elegantly,
Even on the terrace of earth and hell,
That would always provoke fulfillment.

With the above sky,
We were never meant to be,
We met but had to relinquish,
With gigantic sorrowful soul and desperation.

The departure cracked down my chest,

For we are never running into one another,

I heart fully pray to the almighty God

Please, let us encounter each other in the territory of
paradise.

Life of An Orphan

Left to drown in disguise by his parents,

Stands alone in the cruel world,

Learned to live with hunger,

Sometimes submitting the breath to death,

Heart fraught with despair when sighted,

The friends together with their parents,

Well makes it impossible to live,

But up to grow, for he wanted to,

Prove the world that,

Nothing can erase the growth of bravery,

Though alone, gathered the pieces of a dream,

Dreams that,

For it is deeply rooted, in his life

May he be the path we take.

Women Empowerment

Though we existed as an angel,

The cruel society avenged us as devils,

Let's wear lion eyes, stepping paws forward with wide-
opened jaws,

Growl and growl, let's stand forth.

The grace we held didn't matter,

What counted was their mysterious myth,

Give those owl's nature a hefty kick,

Let's not be their susceptible prey.

With generated misconceptions, we are inferior to the
mud,

Like a fearless eagle wandering the space,

Let our wings take as high as the sky could,

With picky eyes down to earth.

The society's tricky trap, let's never reap into,

Instead, reserve the tiger's skin with bravery,

We are capable of earning it,

Both tenderness and immunity ourselves.

Devoid of our validity, the world would convict,

Yet, we ultimately are the glimmers,

Deny being a caged bird with a solitary passion,

Twinkle and twinkle with the heavenly stars without
getting consumed.

With god's consideration, we are elegant throughout,

And, a being with perpetual wisdom though had to bear a
child,

Like a kangaroo, we shall shelter them,

It doesn't render us vulnerable but it's just an extra
obligation we are offered.

Out of different society's fallacies, let's be awake, girls

From generated ancestors, who became creators, let's be
superstition destroyers.

Goodbye For New

A long sigh of

Relaxation,

The year of crisis came to an

End,

It provoked tragic

Miserably,

Challenging the gifted

Life,

Of those innocent humans,

Many of them lost their precious

Vitality,

And they are found nowhere

Today,

The year fetched more memories with

Anguish,

Then the memories of

Pleasure,

The year lent us a mask to

Wear,

Ultimately, those masks remained as

Scars,

Still thousands of

Hearts,

Yet, the coming year of success and

Prosperity

I wish,

The fortunate it would

Bring,

Let those lost souls of the

Year,

Rest in peace,

And brings adequate

Essence,

To those who are still

Breathing,

Let's prepare to battle the

Hardship,

With much self-awareness and

Union,

I wish you a happy new year of

Contentment

One Day, If I Lose My Sight

One day, or another day, the subsequent day,

If I lose my precious sight that day,

I won't be able to catch a glimpse of those beauties,

Or glance at it, staring at me with glories.

Extensive darkness will surround me with the world still in
the glow,

Yet, I have to endure it without a show,

Meanwhile, the glint of the sun will join the night without
a moon,

But to others, the sorrow that I hold will be still unknown.

I will be still alive, but dead inside,

For I will realize, that everything is blank and empty,
besides

The grief I could endure myself,

With the starvation to smile itself.

I will aspire to walk but only with a stick,

I will hear their voices around but not their expression
with a pleasing trick,

The bird may reassure me with her melodic songs,
But will never get to enjoy her classical dances in throngs.

So, If you detect me around someday,
Do not pay me with your sympathy,
But say it, "it's her fate",
And if anyone asks, say to them "it's already too late".

A Frightful Night

Unbroken silence prevails,

In the gloom of midnight shadow,

Moon still with the gleam,

High in the sky,

Surrounded by odd clouds,

Giving a scary sigh,

Mighty winds grant a fearsome ebb,

Which even made far off leaves,

Fall on your house roof,

That gives you a dreading feel.

When all creatures close their eyes,

With the rise of dullness,

Owls remain with loose eyes,

Hearing the pace of ghosts and spirits,

That they crawl from here to there, everywhere,

Craving to bite the flesh you have,

Leaping and hopping,

To see the head of the human once outside the window.

He gazes you through your slight hole,

The whole night, he hangs around,

Near your window, above your bed,

Just to bite you.

The sleepless night,

Turns into a frightful night,

If you catch his eyes at midnight

You will be dead meat.

Oh! Mighty God!

Oh! Mighty God
I have stood here for hours,
My knees are wounded,
For this, the last chance I beg you.

Forgive me for all I have committed,
Though it was not worth mentioning,
Let me praise you with forthcoming,
And retain the last bet.

I forgot to breathe realization,
Was only bound with missteps,
Couldn't make up for me with,
This time, let me amend my fate

I know, I am acting insane here,
With my painful hands pleading,
I'm certainly holding internal prayer,
Do not allow me to go down.

Oh! Mighty God!
With your strength of blessing,
Grant me to give you delight,
And step upright for the best.

Confession

As you stared at me,

My heartbeat faster than usual,

With your shiny pupils,

I could see your head incline,

I trembled with nervousness,

Which I could not control

My utmost shyness,

For a moment I got unconscious,

Because I found

You were only precious.

My Brother, My Friend

You were my only friend, who was vivid and bright,
Sometimes this governed us to continuously fight.
We were like Tom and Jerry,
But when you fell, I rushed in hurry.

That playground we spend all days,
With entire curiosity starting from those golden rays.
Sometimes I pretended to be tired,
But still, you held my hand, and together we discovered.

With your little brain, operated as matured,
Knew every little thing, which even made mom surprised.
You shared with me your single chocolate,
And even your fruits from your cute plate.

Old days persisted to be great,
Created tones of unforgettable memories that will never repeat.
For us, the future was undetermined,
But that inquisitiveness kept us questioned.

Now, we are grown,

Getting apart is what makes me frown.

But what makes me comfortable,

It's seeing you grow with your courageous effort.

Hidden Agony

If you can reclaim your contentment

When I am entirely gone,

I can go off

Just hugging a gigantic smile,

Though, everything arose

Unexpectedly with expectations,

In this survival of living and dead.

Do not fiddle with others' hearts,

Betrayal shall not be forwarded.

Though I received that affection,

Betrayal is still with me,

within the reflection of you,

Salty tears fall,

Those memories have

Purely turned into its thorns.

Many days have gone by,

Yet, those memories,

My heart gets pricked and

Still can't hold it,

Neither I can forget

Nor revive it.

Butterfly

I fly high,

In the space,

Below the blue sky,

Wandering,

Regardless of the trend,

With mighty trust

On my delicate wings,

Exactly to peek at terrific beauties.

Why I Hide Within

Though it's exclusively tough,
Hiding sorrow within myself
Is what I perpetrate,
But I speculate
It's still tough to explain.

Sometimes,
Concealing within myself,
Lends me an incredible relief,
Still,
It wholly seizes my contentment,

You cannot comprehend
My awful grief,
Even if you discern it,
You cannot handle it,
When salty droplets oozes out
Down my cheeks,
Only I can tolerate them.

It complicates me to loosen,

My lips and smile,

Yet, I strive to forget everything,

Just everything,

And give this present a joyful knock.

With this miserable gain,

I am unfortunate,

I fear this realistic being,

It lets me encounter myself to toil again.

Instead,

I believe in those creative natures,

They do not demand,

While I precisely weep in their shoulder

Dwelled Hope But Lost Love

At first sight itself,

The Bell of my heart rang

When my eyes suddenly met yours,

It was meant to be love,

Yet I didn't know somehow,

The feeling it gave me

Was entirely delicate.

I started playing with the

Ebb of winds

For a moment,

I realized myself not walking

But with a jump in my steps,

Vocalizing my utopian songs.

I never forecasted the world of sorrow,

But was possessive

With glossy future with you,

I subsisted with the air you took out
And visualized I took it in.

I was unknowingly cheerful,
Though I didn't know
Why I was,
Everybody saw me altered,
While I whispered them all
Out of a smile.

With those blissful ways,
I felt I am waiting
But could not even figure out
To whom I was,
I was hoping but I didn't know which one
The days went by and hopes vanished.

Those attractive eyes deceived me,
It hired me to follow the hell
With an unusual win,
Though I tried to ignore it,
I was completely lost in the charm,
And ended with an unfortunate will.

Empty World

A sense of feeling adequate and inadequate,

The tentative expression of one which includes sadness
and fear,

A joy, a chill, and excitement,

Everything that stands is temporary.

The things that belong to you,

The people who stays tighter to you,

The extensive wealth you gained,

Everything will be driven one day.

Nature around you is not fixed,

It's not substantial and unreal,

It is one's illusion of the environment.

That will prove empty.

Efforts revived for individual's existence,

Yes, for happiness, stability, and prosperity,

Although brings meaningful living,

Yet, those security and charity bring just an illusion in the
end.

We cannot forbear the truth,

The non-existence of self,

A feeling of fortunate and bewildered,

Thus, this grand truth has to be grasped.

Dark Hour

In the dark hour of my life,

Sun seems to set in the west,

The moon I longed for became dimmer every night,

The affliction of ignorant just remained.

In the dark hour of my life,

That thorny path appeared,

The path that has to be endured with tears,

It got to swallow all the happiness.

In the dark hour of my life,

It dragged me to the edge of the world,

The more I was afraid of being abandoned,

The more I was pretentious.

In the dark hour of my life,

Those who came, they went easily,

Those who stayed, hardly understood,

The law of life is rock, it punished me hard.

In the dark hour of my life,

I was unfortunate, I lived in muddiness,

confusion to identify gave me madness,

With complete grievous feeling.

In the dark hour of my life, I tried to be the light,

Like a burning candle,

Which will eventually die,

There is where I am!

Emotion

My heart cried but my eyes didn't,
The contentment I wanted was absent,
I wanted to run and scream,
Because that dream was in my bloodstream.

I wanted to be in the world of silence,
All the turmoil I had to go with was endurance,
My life was in the mode of pause,
This was all my cause.

My eyes lingered empty,
What my companions had was just sympathy,
My lips searched to smile,
That was when my emotion was unstable.

The path I walked got smaller,
In hot summer, I felt a cold mid-winter,
I was left in solitary,
Every day I dwelled was illusory.

When the night approached, it reaped longer,
I just desired this world to end faster,
Crescent moon, I yearned existed behind the mount,
Whatever my feeling is non-significant beyond bound.

What my heart lusted was not despair,
It made me scared and fear,
In mid-night, I woke up with a nightmare,
Anyway, this has become so familiar.

Mad Hope

With gifted sun, under the blue sky,

I wish to fly as high as I could above the cloud,

With those wings,

Precisely to discover how earth reveals to me,

When the twilight arrives,

I stand with all my hope, I wish,

With the stars, to twinkle and twinkle,

And droop around the affectionate crescent moon.

With those impressive fishes,

I lust to swim willingly,

Uncovering oceanic elegance,

And it's the deepest version that has ever existed.

When the moment enters into hardship,

I prefer to be that one,

Who she could eradicate all the agony that has befallen,

And be an unknown miracle creator.

Child's Fantasy

Though he stands prepared, all he can be is capable of
imagination,

With a closed eye, he gets into his daydream,

For a moment, smiles radiantly under the rays of
hallucination,

With plenty of fantasies, gets into the world of delusion
just while holding, in his hand a creamy ice cream.

Adequate direction enlightens a child's brain,

That's when he tries to be alone and count those
microscopic stars,

He discovers and becomes everyone's captain who he tries
to sustain,

With stars, he then envies becoming an astrologer.

With immense encouragement, he learns to be courageous,

He gets motivated and drags his illusionary dreams to
reality,

When the boldness lies within him, he becomes more
cautious,

The more he walks attentively, the more his life will get
stability.

Man of Never Give Up

Fate offers grieves to everyone,
That everyone hauls their tears within,
Life lends us susceptible routes to live,
Some drops away leading further.

How do you see me? Solid and tall?
The manly look I deliver,
But I am unexpectedly broken inside,
The disease "cancer" let me drop to the floor.

Either do I blame God?
Or to my parents?
Darker days followed me to the edge,
Life was rougher than anyone could speculate.

I crawled along and squeezed myself,
The world seemed darker even when the rainbow was
present,
The road seemed broader as I walk,
But I could not hear a bird singing.

The motive that lay inside me was impossible,
But I followed my heart that endorsed me,
I woke up with expectations,
The decision I took was never to step back.

I believed in the worth coming,
I forgot to blame anyone,
Instead kept on thanking almighty God,
For all, I could make this possible.

I kept my God above me,
Accepted all the blessings I deserve,
I ignored those unbearable tears,
And joined my companions with laughter.

Everyday improved as I climbed harder,
Now, I have proved to be better,
I could see hope and inspiration everywhere,
I chose to hold this for a longer period

One Day

The day will come
Ashes I will become
My scent will be blown away
When I am entirely gone away.

My presence will be only felt by special ones
In the alter, offering me everyday wines
Their mind will get filled with our incredible memories
But it will be late and their heart whimpers.

Near ones will reassure my dear ones
When I vacate them with swollen eyes
They beseech with light and candles
They will wish me my peace in bundles.

After a year, they cannot remember
When all they had to endure cold December
My visual will fade away in their mind
It will glide with gently flowing wind.

By then, I will be with those stars
I will gaze at them healing their scars
I will glimpse them, smiling
With their mood, singing.

Broken

I hide my cries within me

With the light,

The scars you created

Lingered inside me,

But with the arrival of twilight,

The pillow perceived my sorrow,

You are that mysterious soul,

Though I craved it,

It's gone and never found.

No Tomorrow

Everybody said

Tomorrow is just next,

But tomorrow never existed,

And that's how everything

Ended on "Today",

Cultivate " Today" with your

Purity of heart,

Enrich the world's core

With your unmeasurable kindness.

Walk Forward

I walk steadily to reach my farsighted destination,

with comprehensive enthusiasm,

It provokes me with enormous positive intention,

Which lets me stimulate myself with optimism.

Numerous challenges I overcome,

Those thorny paths I crawl,

Many people on the way, come,

But I walk in silence without a loud growl.

For only I know, I am ample of determination,

The reasonable example I prefer to become,

To this world, to cover with effective decoration,

And a decent human, not a human of troublesome.

If you accomplish a certain goal, give yourself a reward

Goals are concrete and hard-worked hard work to walk
forward

My Lost Father

His presence made us feel safe,

For we believed, he was incredibly bold.

He was the great companion in this miserable life,

When things got harder and closed, he was the one who
was to unfold.

With his morality, I grew,

It was positively evergreen,

I am the only fortunate one I knew,

And he was the precious men of his children.

The dusk still prevails within,

Yet, it cannot be cleared,

But in every way with your courageous words, I win,

And with your generous heart, I am never disconnected.

Memories With My Kitten

I saw you on that day, sitting lonely on the thorny paths,

Dilemma lingered in you, could not ask anyone for help
but just remained taking a sunbath.

I realized people walking on that identical road had a cruel
myth.

But I believed, even with creatures to have compassion
and faith.

You were as tiny as a chicken head,

I held you in my palm, you shivered but I promised to be
your maid,

After that turn of complete golden rays, I showered you,
for my parents which were stupid,

And had a warm night together, when the dark was frigid.

My affection grew even with your shiny eyes,

When I was isolated, I chose to be with you forgetting all
the miseries,

Feeding you became my passion at all times,

And I never forgot to buy you biscuits even during school
times.

When the light was above us, lustrously,

Under the big trees, we played with gently falling leaves,
peacefully.

I chose to carry you on my shoulder while visiting that
massive field of maize, dramatically,

And that's when I wished to crave for you permanently.

I didn't have friends, butwhichpresence in thissubstantial,

I never had to wear teary eyes because you were only
elemental.

Now, you are that cute kitten, you have become so
influential,

And for my heart, you are as always essential

Metaphor of Water

The water has distinctive magnificence from the elevated
blue sky,

Its cleanliness refreshes between early morning with its hot
tea,

It also relaxes the tough mind with its whispering flows
when there are discerned elegant birds over the fly,

Yet, their direction of flow like a snake is honestly to the
sea.

As Water is a gift to humanity,

For we should realize that it's a blessing from above,

Water serves without any judgment but with humility,

So men should perpetuate willingness and love.

The water has distinctive magnificence from the elevated
blue sky,

Its cleanliness refreshes the early morning with its hot tea,

It also relaxes the tough mind with its whispering flows
when there are discerned elegant birds over the fly,

Yet, their direction of flow like a snake is honestly to the
sea.

Water is the epitome of selflessness,

It gives itself to all creatures without payback as
compensation,

Men should learn from this and withdraw from selfishness,

On Earth, let us operate towards the welfare of everyone's
composition.

Water is as pure as milk,

Which carries away all the impurities with its holiness,

It flows down hugging all the valleys with its calm walk,

Devoiding the notion to face back but forwards with mute
boldness.

Water is a faithful mirror,

For it reflects the true nature,

As the night approaches with moonlight, it reassures us
with the rev of stars,

Without the reality of water, there won't be the creation of
a graceful atmosphere.

Let us consider water as the earth's plumbing system,

It falls on soil with almighty's mission,

To be fed on the earth's surface and should be considered
a genuine gem,

Hence, the thirsty planet gets gentle with free of tension.

With the Implantation of water's character in one's heart,

You will only know the melody of harmony to impart.

Gone Days

It was a glorious summer,
When I stayed with my grandmother,
She has a kind feather,
She fed me a sweet cucumber.

My grandfather was a tremendous believer,
He never left me behind when he went to gather,
All the cattle from the jungle,
All I had was to mingle.

Elegant traditional house surrounded by evergreen banana trees,
I could see, below the roof exquisite buzzing bees,
Those little sparrows are seen,
In that verdant chili garden.

The fatty pig was raised,
Picking peach for her made me interested,
One day, grandpa brought a goat,
I suggested if goat can wear a raincoat.

Every sundown, we assembled near a warm fire,
They were the great teller of adventure,
With those fascinating stories, I obtained advice,
I was left with a golden choice.

Don't Judge Me

I wriggled in everyday routes,
My interior sanity died thousands of times,
I shed an ocean of tears,
You know, you are not prone to judge me.

Your judgment doesn't render me inferior,
With god's consideration,
I am not compelled to be,
I know, you assess me by my reality,
Not with the intentions,
I encircle within.

Your criticism doesn't implicate me,
Your sympathy doesn't simulate me,
My ears protest to your
Mouthful complaint,
I am simply proud of myself.

I am crowded with mistakes,

At times,

You guide your dirty finger at me,

You will ripe like me,

You are not perfect, so not me.

Your encouragement,

I don't appeal,

The further you insult me,

Furthermore, I will shine,

With those scars, I am still elegant,

For I admit, " Because of me, I am

For who I am today.

Choice

As soon as you step this soil,

Make sure you do not slip away

With somebody's oil,

But you have to choose the right ones to avoid needless
turmoil.

Life furnishes multiple intentions,

You need to walk forward with a positive classification,

For all knows, it brings pure clearification,

At times, you are dragged to the province of dilemma,

Your stage and your age grants you perform superfluous
drama,

If you can't handle it cautiously, that's when it will burst
like a volcano's magma.

Catching the right way leads to your determined
destination,

You are mindful, that you are getting peoples' recognition,

You are identified as capable and eventually become a
satisfactory illustration.

My King

A courageous spirit you possess,

But there your heavy heart,

I could feel.

You wear a heavy crown,

But you don't express your strenuous time.

You are a heavenly sun,

I do not fear facing the next elegant morning.

You are that crescent moon,

Even in times of emergencies and infections.

You are champion of compassion,

For all knows,

You are a complete source of encouragement.

You distribute heavenly wisdom,

With enormous care and concern.

Diwali

Home with enormous lights,
Invites tremendous blessings of might,
From twilight till subsequent morning light,

The light welcomes the beginning,
With those incredibly dedicated songs, proudly singing,
Holds the purity of night while enjoying.

Excitement and pleasure is sighted in everybody,
The flint's of glow itself makes everybody,
Receive and impart blessings considering himself
somebody.

Festival of light in a year,
Comes and goes with no gear,
But leaves only heavenly prayer.

Move Forward

Static life pays you zero product,
It gives no fostering and no gain,
As it moves straight with no pain,
It leads to unremembered conduce.

Undaunted feeling pulls you down,
You will realize life is arduous,
Tough time will arise to promulgate in life,
And many queries run but can't answer it.

Self-decision matters in one's life,
A heart can decide what can be done for deal,
Great motivational inspiring talks can heal,
but one's mindful choice should deal.

Charity and good memories will flourish,
Dancing memories begins with a single step.
A smile that attaches with a fabulous feeling,
It defines a vivid meaning in one's life.

Get into troubles and get into emotions,

Receive criticism and be the loser,

Also, be the solution and understand the feeling,

Let the charity begins and gets into improvement,

This can imperceptibly ripe into success.

Raze the sluggish sense,

Get into sensible movement,

Forbear the problems and tackle them,

So, why not lead a dynamic stated life?

Respect is Being Ethical

In a world, you live in,

Both creatures and natures are preciously present,

They occur with earth's creation,

Yet, deserve human's respect.

In a society, you reside in,

Everyone's connection is knitted,

You evolve as a part of a single-family,

Here, morality addresses more than enough.

Self-respect, you need to gain,

For yourself to be the men of dignity,

The more honorable you discover in yourself,

The further you know, " I should respect them".

Admiration and appreciation grows within the respect,

For you know, it provokes the healthy relationship,

In which you deliver your integrity,

And without alarm, can receive numerous blessings.

Being respectful denies discrimination,

For you realize, respect is being ethical,

Natural birth to peace and prosperity occurs,

Hence, it lets the world revolve with its internal elegance.

Dear Spectacles

Without you, I see no world,
The nearer you are,
The better my heart feels.

Devoid of you, I tumble down,
The distant you be,
I want to follow you.

In absence of you, someone pushes me hard,
The more I suffer from anxiety,
The more I feel scared.

Without you, someone screams at me,
The more they point, I feel insulted,
The sound creeps me.

Without you, I can't utter a word,
When the shady appears, I serve silent,
The dumb in me makes me mad.

Without you, I am sightless,

The more I walk, twilight follows me to the end,

Thank you spectacle, all I have is you!

World of Ecstasy

Once I was in a world of gloom,

With that heavy fall, mostly I endured,

But your entrance gave me an elegant bloom,

Now I am with you, like a dream destined.

With you, this realm restores undefined hopes and
inspirations,

Regardless of the measurable presence of miseries,

I foresee our world with god's consideration,

Like Romeo and Juliet, creating a glorious love stories.

I'll let the cosmos know, the purest rapture of our
affection,

Yet leaving society's hostile judgment aside,

For we know, we are walking in an obligated destination,

And that's what our fate has to decide

Life Ain't Easy

Life is a never-ending journey,

Thousands of eyes lie on the road,

For this, now people judge by money.

And small misstep is created into broad.

Turn deaf ear to the negative world,

Everyone carries hidden reason,

And accept the optimistic judgment, by generating a
pleasant life remaking fold.

It's for oneself, just need to follow the heart, strength, and
compassion.

Be positive, being judged is an extraordinary feeling,

After the sunset, night welcomes,

You build the courage to step ahead of them with great
making.

But without heed, fresh morning becomes.

Mom

A mom gifted to me, no one can obtain,

Like the ecstasy of blooming spring,

Even in autumn, I see in you,

Until the sky falls over, I am with you.

You were there when I unlocked my eyes to catch a
glimpse of this fantastic world,

You were there when I initially felt this soil,

You were there when I primary uttered,

And you are yet with me.

Your caring sense, no one can bestow,

Your innermost concern, no one can forward,

Your devotion, I can purely feel,

Your prosperity, rely on me.

With you, I see cosmic beauties everywhere,

With you, I never get exhausted to count stars,

With you, I never understand miserable,

Because you are only an incredible being.

Because of you, today I am here,
Because of you, I am somebody,
Because of you, I am constantly on a smile.
Let me say, you are my angel.

The period has generated changes,
Yet, my heart pertains to you,
And it saddens me for, I am far away,
Still, you are always connected to me.

Along The Road

With the morning chirps of those realistic insects,

We walked our steps deliberately,

The entire nature greeted us with its inner sense,

I was incredibly delighted with your presence.

When those golden rays penetrated through tall trees,

I could see in you, a heavenly shine,

I quietly put my hands around my mouth and asked those
gentle breeze to strike,

So I could see your gentle smile with its mild flow.

As we walked farther,

I thanked the high sky for the rain,

We shared our warm blood under that yellow umbrella,

And witnessed magnificent rainbows above the hilly
mountain.

It was just you and me, striding,

Hazardous creators were non-existent there,

Birds added warmness to my heart,

When your hands are on mine.

The day was full of affection and devotion,

With both compassionate heart and nature,

I stared over my shoulder and appreciated nature for being
with us,

And glared up to the huge sky for our reasonable love.

Dusk

Your soul with gigantic darkness,

With the zipped secret, you conceal inside,

Your head is low, like a giant wave holding deep down the
ocean,

With immense fear it collects.

Reveal me your dusk, I will be your fresh dawn,

I can make the sunrise with no eclipse,

Your fear will tear, and walk the midnight,

The assault in your head shall be driven.

Your passion is taking you alone near the beach,

The evil spirit is overcoming your essence.

Your emotion is rolling like a marble,

You are scared to interrupt.

Disclose me your dusk, you shall cheer up,

I will be that, one to avert nasty spirits,

You are already rolled,

But let us push in a pleasant gap.

Be With Me

With every sunrise,

I expected to see you beside me,

But it just brought the darkness

As I kept on waiting.

Far from me,

I watched the moon,

I pampered my heart along with it.

The wind blew so gently,

It kindly touched my cheeks,

What shall I do?

My mind blew with its kindness,

The reflection of you never hesitated to emerge,

Every night passed on your image.

When the daylight begins,

My hand searched yours to hold,

It just let to crawl those unforgettable memories.

With the shadow, I walked,
With nature, I felt,
With maturity, I thought.

I wished you were around me,
Every time I watched back,
But my heart could not stop getting pinched.

I came back and longed for you,
But It was all the emptiness,
With that memory memories.

Let me go with the flow, give me your partial woe,
Please, stare me around you,
I am ever with you!

September Rain

With intense sleep, I opened my eyes in the morning,

I pushed my hand above my head to open my curtained window,

The gigantic mass dropping sound I heard,

A fresh wind blew over my ears,

The heavy September rain was tumbling,

I could see green grasses down,

delightedly receiving the rainfall,

Dancing in the gently blowing breezes,

I could see my blossoms with enormous charm accepting the slight rain,

boosted by the winds on the windows.

I could not see the blue sky,

reassuring songs sung by the birds,

But the massive drop of September fall,

It was all foggy above the ground,

I realized nature is sharing her sorrow because he could not hold it any longer.

She gushed her sorrow,

Just to bring the clear blue sky,

Holding back her desperations could bring fog for all
times,

She has her reason to fall,

But her fall made September fascinating.

Waited You

My love,

I called you

You didn't seem to answer,

I texted you,

Still, you didn't reply to me,

You seem to forget me

Our relationship, our promise, our bet, and our dreams,

I can feel only the thorns,

The thorn of dry roses,

I was already in autumn without the recognition,

The feeling of loneliness

It creeps to me every minute,

When, I think deep down,

my salty tears tend to roll down.

This distant relationship,

Is it trustworthy or not?

We had a golden relationship,

I would always treasure,

The great memories we created together,

I still remember, we walked the endless journey,

But somehow it got ended.

Please come back,

I will wait for you until the world ends.

My Cruel Fate

At times, the most awaited moment succeeds,

Then and there, thunder starts to growl and roar,

I get horrified but I believed in faith,

I tolerated it and I relinquished.

Honoring moment I wanted to commemorate,

It was all on me, the bird sang a sad song,

What I earned was an awful heart,

I was destined to get hurt.

I wanted to be adored,

But what I discovered was we are not implied to be,

My heart terrorized and pricked,

No one accompanied me but heavy rain did.

I am not lady luck,

For all know, I earn misery and grief,

I wanted to whimper but I accept it,

You are cruel, my fate!

Eternal Optimist

Create a sense, "I am very strong",
Do not let evil disturb your peace of mind.
Get up with your confidence,
Grow up with certainty.

Think positive, act positively.
work for best, expect for best.
Be enthusiastic about success,
Forget the mistakes but realize them.

You are an optimist, do not create time to criticize,
you are humble, you are a prosperity giver.
You give smile and take smile.
You became others' strength and happiness.

Create a positive mood and morale,
With a positive set of purity, you Inhale.
Help the old, get the blessing,
Advice the young, give a blessing.

Once you are an optimist,
Negative emotions are away from you.
The more you flourish the prosperity,
You will live long.

Optimism prepares you to deal with failures.
it will build resilience and persistence.
It will aid you in hard situations,
Let you through fulfillment and satisfaction.

Letter

Hey! My love,

I am sending you a piece,

Please open and graze,

I uttered all my love with its fragrance.

What my heartfelt, I jotted it down,

My feeling gave me a crown,

Each of the alphabets is aligned for you,

All my happiness is there with you.

To you, this heart belongs,

There you exist, then I do,

Like smile brings satisfaction,

you are my compassion.

Let's make this love fascinating,

with each other's enthusiasm,

Let's carry one soul,

And get rusty together.

My heart sings in your name,

I huddled my love for you,

You are my only seed,

That will be cultivated in my heart.

Dassain

Hindus most awaited festival of autumn,

And the celebration of Goddess Durga's conquest against
Mahisasur,

The victory of Lord Rama over Ravana is celebrated,

It's the festivity of good over evil.

The day of prosperity and unity,

Families get to centralize together,

The Day of relaxation,

After long months of work.

The day starts with the tika ceremony,

A bunch of excitement is glimpsed in everyone,

Preference for new clothes,

With smiles and laughter that prevail on everyone's lips.

The day is enormous of achievement,

With the blessing of goddess Durga,

The day is of immense satisfaction,

With the family and relatives throughout.

The unique culture it illustrates,

Hindus can't ignore it,

The devotion is generated,

With the accomplishment of tremendous blessing.

Wedding Anniversary

I could grasp the fresh wind blow early in the dawning,

With those cypress trees waving nature with their flexible
buds.

When the sturdy sun wriggled above the mountain with a
graceful smile,

It brought extraordinary consensus because it was your
day.

May your affection be stable,

And let your dream flow concurrently like a river,

May your tenderness exist as always,

Because you are a heavenly couple.

May your devotion to each other, stay as long as the sky is
there,

And let your hands hold each other as long as there is the
presence of soil,

May the golden rays cheer up your gentle smile,

And let the moon accompany you altogether, to conquer
the dullness.

The most privileged pair I have ever discovered,

Even the stars enlisted to twinkle with you.

You stand with high dignity,

With great pride, I wish you a happy anniversary.

Loser

Dusk pursued him with everyday nightmares,

His foot, lead on sprinting away, with total carelessness,

Carrying scattered dreams in the air,

And clenching desolate surroundings.

A cruel fate he delivers, head lowly down,

Missing, the courage he should clutch,

Tones of fear he compiles,

And the unknown secret he disguises within.

Absence of regret he counts,

For he knows, "he is doomed",

Fortunate days are gone,

With all his cause,

Speculating himself, " Nothing is getting better".

Let Me Be

Let me be your chair

When you withstand life is unfair

Let me be your bed

When you get exhausted

Let me be your pillow

I will perceive all your sorrow

Let me be your journey

I will never betray

Let me be your spectacle

I will accompany you when you are in obstacle

Let me be your water

You do not need to run farther

Let me be this delicate wind

I will stimulate your heavy mind

Let me be the faraway moon

You will renounce your day-long frown

Let me be the star

I will be your bliss maker.

Music

You have a marvelous rhythm,

My ears starve to listen to you,

Though my voice doesn't fit to sing next to you,

My heart can't wait to dance to that melody,

And my head keeps on nodding.

You pour the deep ocean soothing mean,

I get lost regardless of the environment,

You make me fly with those fantastic clouds above the
dramatic hills,

With luxurious golden rays next to emerge,

I cannot interrupt my feeling.

With you, I am not deserted,

You teach me to celebrate alone,

Even under thunderstorms with heavy hail,

I invent my Castle world,

Only with you.

My sorrows scurry away,

You transform my earliest moods.

I disregard the worldly chaos,

But I trip beyond this mud alone,

I ride in your carol.

You heal my scars when I am dreary,

When all disappears, you effort me,

I choose to be near the stream,

With you, prevailing beside,

With your hymn longing in my heart.

Under The Blue Sky

Under the blue sky, above the blue ocean
The green earth stayed evergreen
People were total peacekeeping
While the bird sang its song.

The river's sound was so peaceful
And its flow was meaningful
Fishes danced swiftly
When the mighty wind blew over fiercely

People were found in green valleys
Pretty little houses were built with tree galleries
Mothers were seen nurturing their children
When men were already in the hunting garden.

All these were in the past
Once when our ancestors were a priest
The priest of nature and its beauty
When they held nature's responsibility.

With peoples' greedy desires
Trees are cut down and burnt into the fire
Timbers are extracted, industries were built
Their wants and needs were quilts

Ice from hilly mountain ran down
The flood washed away the hometown
The cool winter brought summer
This is what, climate change can answer.

Friendship

Ohh, my ship of friends,
I caught you then and there,
Meeting you was a miracle,
Your heart with an open chest was near.

Let's stroll together until the dusk succeeds,
And conquer the frigid night until the dawn,
Let's attend the morning chirp of insects,
And feel the neat dew of meadow.

When sorrow stands before us,
Let's feel together with the crescent moon,
When prosperity attains,
Let's choose the sun to smile beside.

Let's swim the vast ocean,
With those brilliant fish,
To achieve the other angle,
Let's grab our hands right and tight.

Let's build strength,

When the rocks tumble, let's run,

I will be there with you, don't abandon me,

You are here, I don't crave more.

Blessed Rainy Day

The blessed rainy day imprints the end of the rainy season,

It commemorates an important point in September,

It's the celebration of culture and tradition,

Which is a generated one by the ancestors.

Preserving culture stands in one's heart,

It interprets values, integrity, and morality,

It clarifies our past and forthcoming,

Where the family and society are restructured.

The day starts with a fresh bath with blessed rain,

With a silent prayer in heart, one gets to remove sins with
the dirt,

Everyone enjoys a plate of thumb with family and friends,

It brings tremendous prosperity to them,

Different dishes are prepared for lunch,

Which they do not differentiate each other,

But comes together and enjoy the deliciousness,

Though the rain falls slightly,
People are seen around, they believe it's a blessed rainfall.

Men are fond of archery,
They get to prepare the ground with great excitement.
Boys are seen in Khuru field,
With pride, hanging a Dhar,
Great excitement prevails in their eyes.

Women are the fabulous creature,
They wear delightful dresses and joins,
They present the men with marvelous dances,
And helps them to cheer up with games.

Children are seen lingering everywhere,
They expect flavorful dishes,
Where parents are pleased to feed their children,
The future is seen in their fate, which they have to lead the
culture.

Courage

Courage is withstanding danger with no fear,
It undergoes the hazardous period with roar,
And reaps the right,
With intense fight.

Courage is climbing up every moment you fall,
It bestows satisfaction every time you recall,
With every little subsequent step you take,
That's how your accomplishment will make.

Courage is when you concede it,
You create mistake but comprehend it,
You know how to obtain responsibility,
When your entrance is knocked by opportunity.

By courage, you accumulate strength,
You say "I did it" after a long breath,
By confident you face,
Even in an arduous horse race.

Courage reserves you to hold tight,

Even in the battle of midnight,

You pulls the string when your life is at the edge,

By bravery you bring change.

International Peace Day

September in autumn is extraordinary,

The glint of seasonal graces is seen.

Peace prevails everywhere,

In natures and creatures,

Because September is ample of peace,

It comforts one's impressions.

Peace is bringing progress and prosperity,

Peace is sharing darkness and gaining past,

Peace is assisting others and earning satisfaction,

Peace is allocating equality and strength,

Peace is being polite and thoughtful,

Peace is being courteous.

Peace denies sound of guns and bombs,

But desires relaxing songs by the birds,

Peace denies discrimination,

But desires pure essence,

Peace denies diseases,
But accepts healthy smiles.

Peace lies in one's heart,
A compassionate heart,
Peace lies on the buds of the trees,
Which lingers with a gracious wind breeze,
Peace lies on the flowing streams,
Which creates hustling glamour.

Blessed Autumn

The daylight of autumn serves shorter,

When night length gains until December.

The essence cools down,

And the transition in color is glimpsed in green leaves,

When they prepare to subside.

The sun was high with scattered clouds,

The pleasant breeze touched my feeling,

With those ripening grains in the field,

The face of the ground, covered with fallen leaves,

I saw birds preparing for cold winter.

Autumn stores her unique beauty,

When the season breaks into the exotic countenance of
nature,

I could see fresh vegetables surrounding that traditional
house,

With the hope, nature grabs to begin one day.

People born in autumn are believed to live extended,

I believed it, I met those autumn people,

My heart earned to melt with their kindness,

They didn't differentiate people stepping on the roads,

But kept on delivering their compassion.

Those autumn people were settled there,

With a big heart and expectation,

Their paddy got to ripe in that incredible village,

And they seem to admire this glamorous autumn.

Because I could see extensive smiles in their manner.

Far Away Meadow

In a far-away meadow

As the summer commences

I prefer to be there,

I walk alone every Sunday

Because I have my genuine buddies there,

With the glimmering sunrise, I greet them, "Good morning".

Listening to soothing songs

Sang by the birds,

And the whispering hymn of winds

It gives my ear hope,

Clean stream following down the meadow,

I thank her for not allowing my meadow to dry,

I look up high and wish the blue sky,

The silence prevails there but I adore it,

The green scene makes me crazy,

It gives me an all-natural scent,

I inspect the bugs climbing my clothes

And the bees buzzing in the blooming flower,

I talk to them and ask myself " nature is incredible",

I linger there with all my smiles,

I want to tickle them but I don't,

The flowers are like angels,

It gives me a thriving desire,

As the sun sets, I love the glamorous ending sun rays,

I watch the rays trudging over the mountain,

It reflects me, it all has to come and go,

I wish the evening not to come, but it did,

I gaze them all for last,

I wish them to wait for me,

I wish them good night.

Moment of Time

The sun rises with its magnificent beams that day

It accomplishes to appear the next day

Yet it cannot be reversed

Like the sun, moment tickles every day but at different times.

Each second carries one's thought

Every blink of eyes sorts difference

Every step you take makes sense

Every heartbeat feels it's the moment.

Each minute holds one's memory

Your precious period with family

Your party momentum with colleagues

Each memory flies with time.

Each hour you determine to work hard

Your generosity and fear

Your personality and vitality

All these retain each moment.

Moment clings with time
Moment switches but time don't
Time ascertains the opportunity
What moment does, it grab that opportunity.

My Little Star

When I wanted to wail,

I find no one beside me,

The loneliness takes me far,

but I want to see you, little star.

I quickly open the window,

There I find you, shining far above the meadow,

You are tiny but shiny,

Your smile takes my grief away.

I wait the night to come,

As I watch you, I pray not to end,

You fly from one home to another,

I feel you are calling me there.

You have a motherly moon,

A place you have is a heavenly grown,

My little star, you have whom to hold,

With you, let me come there to play fold.

You are rich, you have glittering friends,

They seem kind with a pure heart like yours,

My little star, come closer,

I want to be with you together.

Memories

The generosity you gave

The kindness you forwarded

And the assistance you awarded

These are all the memories.

Your time spent with family

Your playground with your friends

Your laughter with them

These are all the memories.

When you bunked your class

The scolding your teacher gave

Your pretending and resistance

These are all the memories.

You found your pocket was zero

And learned how to use it after that

When you asked your parents for good

These are all the memories.

Above all, your past is your memories.
All you have to do is cultivate memories.
These memories are your story.
These memories are your joy and laughter

Everyone is busy making their story
In their mind for memories.
memories cannot be reversed
It can be only created.

Tears of Sorrow

My heart feels it stopped beating

My smile seems meaningless

I without notice, walking in the rain in winter

After you stopped keeping me in yourself.

The call I did at first gave me millions of hope,

It was all hurt you gave me.

Still, I upheld your pride.

It completely tore my heart

When you just say you are busy.

You never called me back,

And I waited for you.

It was nothing that I waited for you all along,

But now I knew I was all alone for along.

Since long ago I was completely alone.

I didn't know coz I was busy hoping you would be back.

All I can realize now is

I was as looser as I am.

I can give you what you wanted

And it was all my fault from the start.

The day I caught your love

I was unbelievable towards myself.

But I see the earth is turning upset down.

And I'm already tired of everything

I have nothing to gain from you,

All I have is to wish you thank you

And wish you all the best I can.

I love you.

Since

Since the day you strolled into my ladder of heart

I was no longer myself

I was unconscious, where am I?

I was in search of all in all of your presence.

Since the day you stared at me

I always longed for your impression

Your smile made me crazy

I could even reach to stop the breath

every side of yours honestly made me die.

Since the day you hold my hand

I was already in the ocean of love

The unconditional love I owe

I dreamt infinite goals of us

Regardless of the people I came across.

Since the day you hugged me

I felt I was fortunate

The safer I felt
The more I realized
we are meant to be together.

Since the day you kissed me
I felt we are evergreen plants
The heartbeat faster than normal
Even my heart knew you are only the truth
With you, I decided to ride this world.

Since the day you asked for marriage
I couldn't stop the tears of happiness
My greatest happiness you are
May the almighty knows
You are only my part of every beat.

Humanity

The care, concern, affection,

And admiration,

Humans among breathing creatures

Should put into confirmation,

Not from their screams,

But from the heart and mind,

Realizing, God has creatively

Created only for humankind.

The confidence of feeling and understanding,

Only humans can maintain,

But over the generated years,

Humanity has just remained

As a curtain,

Revealing the dark side wrapping it's a necessity

Still with the absence of regret,

Shame, and guilty.

Humans surrounded by humans
Are judged by humans,
Based on color, caste, gender,
And standard which is inhumane,
Character and behavior didn't matter to them,
But cruelty enjoyed the cruel game.

When the earth is still in the glow,
Why the responsible species are in the
Cruel flow?
Let this blow of oddness go off,
And sow the seed of value, show off!

Let the perception of anger, greed, selfishness, and
Fustration vacate from your nerve,
Instill extraordinary definition in your heart
Then serve,
Commence respecting yourself initially,
Beginning to formulate humanity as a
Religion generously.